Crea Anger Expression

Roger & Christine Day

Brook Creative Therapy

Published by:

Brook Creative Therapy, Brook Cottage, 16 Burnside, Rugby, Warwickshire CV22 6AX, UK

Details of how to order further copies can be obtained by emailing brookcreativetherapy@gmail.com

About the authors

Roger Day

Certified Transactional Analyst, Psychotherapist and Play Therapy specialist

For many years Roger has been a trainer and supervisor specialising in children and families. Now retired, he lives in Rugby, Warwickshire.

Christine Day

European Adult Teaching Certificate, Nursery Nurse Examination Board (NNEB), Diploma in Counselling, Certificate in Counselling Skills

Christine is a qualified nursery nurse. In addition to successfully raising four children, over the years she has added play and creativity specialisms to her nursery skills. Christine lives with Roger in Rugby, Warwickshire.

Books by Roger & Christine Day:

Matryoshkas in Therapy: Creative ways to use Russian dolls with clients
Creative Anger Expression
Creative Therapy in the Sand: Using sandtray with clients

Christine & Roger Day have also published the following books in CD-ROM form:

Body Awareness: 64 bodywork activities for therapy (2008/2011)
Therapeutic Adventure: 64 activities for therapy outdoors (2008/2011)
Stories that Heal: 64 creative visualisations for use in therapy (2011)

Brook Creative Therapy, Brook Cottage, 16 Burnside, Rugby CV22 6AX, UK

Acknowledgements

Our first big thank you is to the many clients, usually adult female survivors of child abuse, who over many years told Roger in therapy that they were so angry they needed a punchbag. Without their honesty and openness about their own need to express anger, Roger would not have pursued the theme of creative anger expression and this book would not have been possible.

We also thank supervisor, trainer and psychotherapist Keith Tudor for introducing the idea of 'anger expression and violence management' in preference to the highly popular term 'anger management'.

Both of us are grateful to the numerous trainees, supervisees and clients in recent years who have told us how helpful they have found creative anger expression. Without their encouragement and support we would not have continued the development of this important but often neglected therapeutic release.

Introduction

General anger work with clients

What is anger? Many people think of anger as out-of-control shouting, fighting, kicking or hitting. Of course, some people allow a release of anger in these inappropriate and even frightening ways. But it is much more than that. *Anger is the emotion that provides us with the energy we need to solve our problems or get what we need – now.* It is an emotion that can lead to calm, rational yet assertive decisions.

One of us (Roger) has written: 'Anger is a release of energy that can help you sort out your problems or protect you from harm' (Day, 2004, page 6). Many people, however, use 'cover-up feelings' (op cit, page 5) to repress their feelings.

In many families, and even in whole societies, expressing anger is not considered acceptable. Roger again: 'There may be good reasons why it wasn't or isn't safe for the child to show their real feelings, but they will need to relearn effective ways to express their appropriate feelings once these reasons are identified and it is safe to express authentic feelings once again' (Day, 2008, page 183).

Bridle and Sweet write that: 'Anger is hot, fiery and powerful. It is also beautiful, motivational and can energise us into action for progress and change' (Bridle & Sweet, 2000, page 33).

Susannah Temple points out that anger is not the same as a person losing his or her temper. She writes: 'Anger is to do with the energy of feeling powerful, and effectively making changes. Loss of temper is to do with outbursts which are the outcome of frustration and helplessness' (Temple, 1993, page 7). When anger is blocked, she believes, it leads to frustration, resentment, a build-up of tension and finally a violent outburst.

It is our belief that expressing anger on a regular basis in safe, appropriate ways can help to diffuse the build-up of anger that often leads to 'violence' in the form of losing temper, shouting, fighting, domestic violence, road rage and other inappropriate and unhelpful expressions of anger. From this we have developed various techniques, detailed in this book, for *expressing anger and managing violence.*

This approach is rather different from the prevalent and highly popular use of anger management. Yet there are some professionals who take a similar line.

Dr Vernon Coleman once ran a stall at a local fête in which people would pay a small amount of money to throw wooden balls at piles of old plates. He writes: 'It was fascinating to watch people's reactions and to see people losing their accumulated aggression. Tired businessmen with weary eyes and slumped shoulders walked away with smiles and spring steps. Harassed looking mums, looking fed up and slightly edgy, left just a touch embarrassed but really rather pleased with themselves. One rather bad-tempered old fellow, who looked like a caricature of a traditional English colonel, arrived with a scowl and left with a merry chuckle . . .

'But if you really feel too embarrassed to do anything quite so obvious, why not try getting rid of your tension and stress by taking part in a strenuous and violent form of exercise? Smash a squash ball around for 20 minutes, hit a tennis ball or a golf ball as hard as you can. You'll feel much better. You may not win any trophies playing that way, but you'll do yourself a power of good' (Coleman, 1990, page 105).

Tom Frazier writes: 'Therapists need to be comfortable with anger and its expression. They also need to share what the deeper feelings and needs are under the anger and, if necessary, be willing to go around the anger to those deeper feelings' (Frazier, 1995, page 128).

The Sound Feelings organisation of Trazana, California, founded by Howard Richman, advocates anger expression. It suggests fives steps to anger expression (Sound Feelings, 2012):

❏ Give yourself permission to express anger
❏ Combine mental and physical effort in anger control
❏ Never hurt others in the process
❏ Totally let go without hesitation
❏ Strive to forgive

Research has shown that suppression of anger can lead to stress, frustration, worry and isolation. Stephanie Rude of the University of Texas assessed the levels of suppressed anger and evaluated the accompanying sadness, worry and fear. She writes: 'Constructive anger expression represents a new direction in emotional expression research, with important applications to clinical work' (Rude, et al, 2012).

There are often objections to anger on religious grounds. For instance, many Christians contend that anger is somehow wrong and sinful. They point to a passage in the Bible that says: 'Be angry, and do not sin. Do not let the sun go down upon your wrath, neither give place to the Devil' (Ephesians 4:26-27 Modern King James Version).

Christian writer Tim Jackson believes this passage does not endorse indiscriminate anger. However, he observes that many people misinterpret the passage as: 'Don't be angry, because it's sin' (Jackson, 2000, page 13). 'Anger and love are not mutually exclusive,' he writes. 'They can be two different sides of the same coin. Righteous anger in a compassionate person can be very productive for the well being of others' (op cit, page 14).

As committed Christians we applaud Jackson's gesture but would go further. All anger (not just 'righteous' anger) that is expressed in a safe, appropriate way is acceptable. Anger that is unexpressed or even repressed is more likely to lead to expression in an inappropriate ('sinful') way.

Former Buddhist monk Thich Nhât Hanh (2001) advocates mindfulness as a counter to anger. He writes:

'Anger is a mental, psychological phenomenon, yet it is closely linked to biological and biochemical elements. Anger makes you tense your muscles, but when you know how to smile, you begin to relax and your anger will decrease. Smiling allows the energy of mindfulness to be born in you, helping you to embrace your anger' (page 27).

Our view is that, while smiling is very helpful for many clients, others have so much repressed anger that creative anger expression seems the most effective way for them to release their anger and move on.

Opponents to expressing anger blame wrong interpretation of Sigmund Freud's theory known as the 'hydraulic model'. The theory is that repression blocks or dams energy, keeping anger from being expressed and leading to neurotic symptoms. Such opponents observe that research on the *catharsis hypothesis,* which has risen out of Freud's theory, has shown that expressing anger and aggression towards others (partners, work colleagues, classmates, etc) fuels more anger rather than lessens it.

One book puts things bluntly. 'Anger is basically a matter of choice. It is determined by your thoughts and beliefs far more than your biochemistry or genetic heritage. Venting anger rarely leads to any real relief or any lasting catharsis. It leads instead to more anger, tension and arousal' (McKay et al, 1989, page 22).

We agree that expressing aggression towards others is unhelpful. The kind of anger proposed in this book generally involves inanimate objects rather than other people or animals. It is our view that this form of expression of anger is safe and healthy. Repression of anger, on the other hand, can lead to problems of digestion, heart disease, raised blood pressure and reduced ability to fight infections.

The authors of the same book make a useful point about people's choice of whether to get angry or not. For the kind of person who gets easily angry in various situations, they suggest the Response Choice Rehearsal (McKay et al, 1989, page 179):

Express specific need: 'I'm feeling . . .'

Negotiate: 'What would *you* propose to solve the problem?'

Self care: 'If . . . goes on, I'll have to . . . . in order to take care of myself.'

Get information: 'What do you need in this situation?'

Acknowledge: 'So what *you* want is . . . '

Withdraw: 'It feels like we're starting to get upset. I want to stop and cool off for a while.'

Many modern transactional analysts advocate anger expression. But it was not always that way. Founder and psychiatrist Dr Eric Berne, who developed the concept of 'racket feelings' (an inauthentic feeling covering up an authentic one), made quite scathing remarks about anger expression: 'Since about 90 per cent of anger is a "racket" encouraged by the Parent [ego state], the real question is "What good does it do to get angry?" It seldom accomplishes anything that cannot be done better without it, and the price is hardly worth paying: four to six hours of disturbed metabolism and several hours of insomnia' (Berne, 1975/1972, page 380).

Jonathan Miller takes the view that understanding and naming the associated emotions associated with anger will help to deflate the exploding balloon of anger. He writes: 'When someone explodes with rage, we can see them deflated and torn once the crisis has passed. Emotion-word lists help clients flatten out the gasbag of anger, because naming something (such as the emotions inflating the balloon) gives you power over them' (Miller, 2012).

We have found consistently that using writing, art and other creative techniques is one of the most effective introductions to anger expression for both individuals and groups of adults, young people and children. By far the favourite art activity has been the Angry Page developed by Margot Sunderland. For copyright reasons we have not included this in the book, but a brief look at how it is used can be helpful.

Sunderland writes that one of the page's major objectives is 'to educate people about the importance of expressing their anger in safe ways as opposed to keeping it inside or swallowing it, which can be damaging both physically and emotionally; or acting it out in ways which are harmful to self and others' (Sunderland & Engleheart, 1993, page 44).

The idea of the Angry Page is to think of someone you are angry with who is affecting you now. It could be someone living or dead. That person is kept in mind as the various sections are filled in. These include drawing the person's face and poking a hole through the paper or rubbing dirt or food on it. It also includes scribbling hard, colouring in red, putting the person in the stocks and drawing tomatoes, rotten apples and custard pies on the face!

When we have used the Angry Page we have always asked clients and trainees at the end what they want to do with their pages. In almost every case they want them destroyed. This varies from screwing them up and throwing them forcefully into a bin, to tearing them into small pieces, to going outside and setting fire to them.

Most adults and children find this form of gentle expression a great initial release. No one is hurt in the process and the client is often able to move on in life less hindered by repressed and unresolved anger.

This book contains a wealth of other creative activities to express anger, within or outside the therapy room, in order to help clients manage their inappropriate violence in the form of words or actions. We hope you enjoy using the activities as much as we enjoyed writing about them.

A word of warning

Creative anger expression by its very nature evokes deep, early feelings. Before you introduce these exercises to clients ensure that they have done enough therapeutic work that they are not tempted to use the activities to harm themselves or harm someone else. If you notice a tendency towards self-harm, stop the activity immediately. The same applies if a client is tempted to hurt you or, in group work, 'accidentally' attempts to hurt someone else.

Anger work with children and families

There are a number of additional points to make for therapists working with under-16s, including families. Anger is one of the most common presenting issues for children and young people and it is useful to have plenty of tools in the therapeutic toolkit for creative anger expression.

It is extremely important that ground rules are clearly established before children are encouraged to express the anger they have within them. First, they must understand clearly that they are not generating anger but expressing what is already inside them. Second, they need to know that what can be done in individual therapy or in the security of a therapy group may not be acceptable in front of others at school or at home. Once these two things are clearly understood, safety rules need establishing.

For several years in therapy groups with children we have successfully used the Anger Rules developed by Whitehouse & Pudney (1996, page 7):

'It's OK to feel angry *BUT*
* Don't hurt others
* Don't hurt yourself
* Don't hurt property
– *DO* talk about it'.

We have become increasingly concerned that the rules are so negatively worded. According to Neuro-Linguistic Programming (NLP), reframing a positive intention is preferable to giving a negative command.

'The way to get rid of unwanted behaviours is not to try and stop them with will-power. This will guarantee they persist because you are giving them attention and energy. Find another, better way to satisfy the intention, one that is more attuned to the rest of your personality' (O'Connor & Seymour, 1990/1993, 131).

NLP Master Trainer Robert Smith explains positive intention in terms of giving instructions to a small child. 'If you say to a child: "Don't drop that tray," he'll hear the last few words. As like as not he will indeed "drop that tray". Putting it into the positive you could say: "Put the tray carefully on the coffee table." Again, he hears the last few words, puts down the tray and nothing is broken or spilt' (Smith, 2000).

As a result of our concerns we have developed our own Anger Guidelines for children based on the idea of positive statements:

Expressing your anger is OK with me

Make sure that you:
❏ Talk about it with a trusted adult
❏ Take care of yourself
❏ Respect other people
❏ Value your things and those of others

For children and young people who favour writing down their thoughts on various feelings, consider Mark Widdowson's simple emotional literacy exercise. The idea is to write headings on separate pieces of paper with words such as: 'I am angry that . . .'

'The young person is instructed to finish each sentence as many times as possible using their own endings, and to rate the intensity of the feeling relating to each feeling statement on a scale of one to one hundred . . . Finishing the exercise on a positive note will help with generating positive associations with emotional literacy work' (Widdowson, 2008, page 147).

Rational-Emotive Behaviour Therapy takes the view that there is both healthy and unhealthy anger. Jerry Wilde writes in connection with children and young people: 'There are times when it is entirely appropriate to feel irritated and annoyed at someone's obnoxious behaviour. In fact, it would be difficult not to be irritated with some situations. This healthy anger is rational.

'However, when the feelings reach extremes such as rage, clients no longer are thinking rationally because these emotional extremes are almost always self-defeating. Also, rage and extreme anger usually are produced by thoughts pertaining to the character of the person, rather than the behaviour in question' (Wilde, 1996, page 55).

Whitehouse & Pudney (1996, page 46) relate this specifically to anger. They invite children to use 'I' statements to say how they feel and what they want. They suggest using what they describe as the 'four-part magic phrase':

'I feel . . . . (angry, annoyed, furious, niggled, etc)
when . . . . (say what happened)
because . . . . (why it upsets you)
I would like . . . . (what you want to happen or change).'

Talking about her personal observation of messy play in the safe environment of the therapy room, Sharratt (2009) writes: 'I feel that if children sense this safety in my play room (my leaf) and have the freedom to let go of their chaos then they will be free to move on to the next stage of their growth, that of an emerging butterfly' (page 13).

Sharratt concludes: 'The mess-making stage is a necessary part of the therapeutic process brought about by permissiveness and trust. Most of my clients have been able to let go, some taking just one session, while others have needed many more. It is also part of the developmental process where the children are given the opportunity to regress to areas that they have missed, mainly sensory experiences' (Sharratt, 2009, page 15).

Finally, be aware that children's anger can be quite frightening. Perhaps this is why most parents stop their children slamming doors or stamping their feet (two highly effective ways of creative anger expression). If you can overcome your own fear in this area you will be able to help your child clients make major changes that can benefit them for the rest of their lives.

Information to use with clients

Anger questionnaire

When you first start working with clients who have suppressed anger it is useful to find out from them their attitudes, actions and fears about anger and its expression. A useful way to do this is through the Anger Questionnaire (see below). This can be given to them for completion at home, or you as the therapist could fill it in using the questions as a form of interview. Either way it is useful to keep the completed questionnaire with the client notes and refer to it as you work with the client using creative anger expression. Pay particular attention to answers that indicate scare around expressing anger. Ensure that in your work with that particular client you take things one step at a time, giving the client plenty of permissions.

Ways to express anger creatively

Many of the creative activities in this book can be used in the therapy room. It is our belief, however, that creative anger expression needs to be a part of day-to-day life, not just for use in therapy. With this in mind we have devised a take-home sheet that you can copy and give to clients (see below). It is probably useful to give it to them after they have had some experience of creative anger expression within the safety of the therapy room. Also, they need to know that what is perfectly acceptable within the therapy room may be considered strange, weird or even crazy at home, work or school. Prepare your clients for the reaction of others. Better still, encourage them to express anger in places and at times when others are not around.

Anger questionnaire
by Roger & Christine Day

Your name: Date of birth:
       Today's date:

How often do you feel angry?

Do you hold in your anger when you really want to express it?

Are there particular times when you feel more angry than others?

What type of things trigger your anger?

How do you feel in your body when you are angry?

What do you do when you are angry?

Are you able to calm yourself down when you are beginning to feel angry?

How do you feel after you've been angry?

Do you think you lose control when you are angry?

21

For you, is being angry good, bad or neutral?

How could your anger be used constructively?

How do other people react when you are angry?

Do you think you are an angry person?

Does your anger help you or is it a hindrance in life?

Ways to express anger creatively
by Roger & Christine Day

Anger is the emotion that provides us with the energy we need to solve our problems or get what we need – now. It is important to recognise that anger needs expressing safely without hurting yourself or other people or destroying things you value. Practise creative anger expression regularly, daily if at all possible. As you express anger in safe ways you will be less likely to lose your temper or take out your anger on other people.

Here are a few ideas for creative anger expression:

❒ **Run fast, pounding your feet on the ground**

❒ **Tear up paper with energy and without smiling**

❒ **Find a place away from everyone else (a park or field, for instance) and shout or scream loudly**

❒ **Buy an inflatable punchbag and release your anger on it**

❒ **Pile some pillows or cushions on the sofa or bed and pummel them**

❒ **Go outside and kick some leaves, grass cuttings or snow**

❒ **Destroy a cardboard box by jumping on it, tearing and smashing it**

❒ **Scribble hard on a piece of paper**

❒ **Draw the source of your anger, then destroy the picture**

☐ Breathe deeply several times

☐ Run on the spot until you are out of breath

☐ Put a favourite piece of music on and dance vigorously

☐ Go to the swimming pool and punch the water or kick your legs with enthusiasm

☐ Squeeze a stress ball so hard your muscles shake

☐ Tense and relax each part of your body until you feel relaxed

☐ Dig the garden with vigour

☐ Jump on plastic bottles to make more room in the recycling bin

☐ Blow up a balloon, then squash it until it bursts

Using a stress ball

One of the easiest ways to express anger is through using a stress ball. These come in various shapes and sizes. Some give more resistance than others. All stress balls have a measure of resistance. Many people are happy if the ball returns to its original shape the moment it is released. Other people love the types of stress ball that squash right down and then slowly return to their usual shape.

The idea is to squeeze the stress ball and put as much anger into it as possible. Then the client keeps up the pressure until his/her arm muscles start to shake. Finally, the client releases pressure on the ball and relaxes. Clients with a lot of anger may find it even more effective to hold the stress ball at arm's length while squeezing.

As with many other forms of anger expression, it is important not to smile. Smiling detracts from a true expression of anger.

We suggest that therapists keep a stress ball handy in the therapy room and encourage clients to use it. Once they get the hang of it they can buy their own stress ball, keep it readily available and use it as often as possible. Not only will it release their anger; it is a great way to build up arm muscles.

Using a stress ball is safe and healthy. Occasionally people will find that their wrists (front or back) become sore. If this happens it is important to straighten the hand when squeezing in order to avoid strain on the ligaments and muscles.

Digging for emotional victory

There are plenty of ways clients can release their anger in the great outdoors. Whatever the weather or season, there is probably some way in which anger can be expressed outside without it affecting other people.

Gardening is a great way to express anger and end up with a better garden as a result. Encourage clients who have a garden or allotment to get a fork or spade and spend time digging vigorously in the soil or removing the deep-rooted weeds. If it isn't the time of year for digging, get them to hoe or rake enthusiastically. If they have a lawn they could cut the grass with enthusiasm, preferably with a retro hand mower, or edge the lawn or rake up the moss.

If clients are not gardeners they could chop or saw wood for a wood-burning stove. They could go into the woods and crunch their feet on old acorns, kick leaves or break small dead branches with their hands or over their knees.

In winter time they could kick snow or make a small snowman and hurl snowballs at it.

In the therapy room you could bring in small branches for clients to break. An alternative is to crush nut shells under foot, then clean them up afterwards. The easiest way to get the shells is to buy some pistachio nuts, eat the delicious nuts and save the shells for anger therapy with your clients.

Tense and release

A great tension buster for clients is to tense and relax various muscle groups in turn. By the time this exercise is finished the client has usually released a large amount of anger. Apart from tensing and relaxing the face, this can be done at work, home or school without other people noticing what the client is doing.

Below is some suggested wording when working with a client in the therapy room. Once clients have learned the approach, they can continue at any time outside the therapy room, whenever they feel the need to release some anger held in their body.

Here is the suggested wording:

Make yourself comfortable and be ready to release a lot of tension and anger in your body.

Focus first on your feet. Tense them up as much as you can. Feel the tension in your toes and the rest of your feet. Hold them tense for five seconds. 1-2-3-4-5. Now relax your feet and feel them relax. Enjoy the experience.

Focus on your legs. Again, tense them up and hold for 1-2-3-4-5 seconds. Relax them.

Now think of your trunk, the middle part of your body. Tense for 1-2-3-4-5 seconds – and relax.

Turn now to your arms. Tense them for 1-2-3-4-5 seconds – and relax them completely.

Think of your hands. Make fists and tense them, being careful not to dig your fingernails into your hands. Hold them for 1-2-3-4-5 seconds – and relax.

Move on to your neck. Tense it up for 1-2-3-4-5 seconds – and relax.

Think now of your head and face. Tense them both up, making the ugliest expression you can think of. Hold for 1-2-3-4-5 seconds – and relax.

Enjoy your relaxed, anger-released body.

Scribbling hard

For this exercise you will need paper and crayons or ball point pens.

Ask clients to think of someone now or in the recent past who they are angry about. They might think they don't have any anger left. They may have forgiven the person for the wrong they have done. But it is likely that even if they don't recognise it, they are carrying some anger about that person.

Make it clear that it's not OK to hurt that person (or anyone else because of him or her), hurt themselves or destroy property. But it *is* OK to have the person's name in mind when they do this exercise.

Give clients some paper. They will need some kind of pad or board to rest on. They then choose a crayon or ball point pen to use. (Felt tip pens are likely to break.)

Invite clients to focus on the person they are angry with or who has wronged them. Encourage them to scribble hard without smiling. Watch in silence. Don't talk to them unless they talk to you. This gives them space to work out their feelings.

When they have finished discuss together what the experience was like for them. Finally discuss what clients would like to do with the scribbled piece of paper.

Drawing what makes you angry

For this exercise you will need paper in various colours and shapes. You will also need felt tip pens, coloured chalks, pencils and oil pastels.

Discuss with clients about using drawing to put their anger down on paper. This will enable them to look at a representation of their anger and put a name to it. This makes the anger more concrete.

Ask clients what they need for the drawing. What kind of paper – black, coloured, white, smooth, textured? Do they want to use pencils, crayons, chalks, felt tips, oil pastels? What colours do they want? Talk about which colours signify anger for the client. Watch clients as they talk about this. Look for the depth of feeling in their face and body language – frowning, grimacing, clenched fist, etc.

When clients have selected the materials, invite them to sit quietly and think before they draw about what makes them angry.

Clients then start their drawing. While they are drawing observe them as they create their picture. Give them space, only commenting if they speak to you.

When clients have finished it may be useful to photograph the picture for your client notes before asking them what they want to do with the picture. If they want to destroy it, discuss together some creative ways of doing that: tearing into small pieces, shredding, stamping on it or going outside and burning it.

Conquering cardboard

For this exercise you will need some old cardboard boxes of various shapes and sizes.

This is a good exercise if you are working with an individual, a family or a therapy group.

Ask clients or client group to think of something that they are angry about. Then invite them to take out their anger on the cardboard boxes. This can be done by kicking or jumping on them, tearing or ripping them to pieces.

Prompt clients to continue until the cardboard has been reduced to tiny pieces.

As the therapist ensure that clients, you and the objects in the room are safe during this process.

Talk together about what the experience was like for your clients. By their using their energy and getting out of breath they have released anger from their bodies.

Encourage them to get old cardboard boxes and kick them around the garden. This can be a wonderful fun exercise for the whole family and will not be seen as weird or aggressive behaviour.

Keeping fit and beating anger

Physical exercises and dancing are a great help physically for all of us who want to keep fit. They are especially helpful for clients who are dealing with anger because they provide an acceptable, fun outlet for creative anger expression.

Whether you are working with an individual or a group, lead with some simple stretches, circling arms and touching toes. Continue with punching the air and other exercises that encourage a more direct expression of anger. Then the client could take over and lead you both in some more exercises. Keep going until you are both out of breath.

Finish with a very vigorous activity such as running on the spot.

Afterwards process what the exercises were like in terms of dealing with the anger that clients have locked up inside.

Explore with clients how they can continue with keeping fit as a way of expressing anger creatively. They might consider taking up a regular sport such as running or playing football. Games such as tennis or badminton are also very helpful. Perhaps the most effective are high energy contact sports such as judo, squash, boxing, rugby and American football.

Dancing is another way to express anger is a creative way that is socially acceptable. Clients can attend classes in every style from ballroom dancing to much more vigorous styles such as zumba and street dance.

Not every therapist can or would want to lead clients in dance in the therapy room. For the nondancers among us, consider playing some lively music and invite clients to start listening to the music and then let themselves express through their body the music they hear. A second stage could be to repeat this activity with eyes closed.

While clients are moving to the music remind them that movement of the body is a useful way to express their anger.

Afterwards talk about the experience and encourage continued use of movement to music at home.

Paper fountain

Most people end up with a lot of unwanted paper in the form of junk mail, free newspapers, used envelopes, telephone directories and much more. Instead of automatically recycling this, it can be used as an excellent source of anger expression – and then recycled!

We keep old telephone directories and other paper specifically for this purpose. Start by showing clients two different ways of tearing a piece of paper. The first is by holding it between thumb and index finger and ripping it gently. This does not help at all with anger. The second way with a similar piece of paper is to hold it solidly in both hands and rip it rapidly and with considerable enthusiasm. In this way just one piece of paper can be highly effective.

A second stage of anger expression using paper is to focus on the source of the anger (possibly with eyes closed) and then rip the paper violently, making a noise with the mouth as the paper is ripped.

This activity is best done by tearing two, three or four sheets at a time. Clients who are extra strong or have a large amount of anger may need to tear more pieces of paper, such as a small section of an old telephone directory.

Encourage clients to keep tearing the paper until it is in very small pieces. You can facilitate this by tearing paper yourself while they engage in this activity.

When all the paper is in small pieces, celebrate with clients together by throwing all the pieces into the air and letting them come down in the form of a paper fountain. (See cover picture.)

The final stage is for clients to pick up all the pieces of paper and throw them into a bin, with enthusiasm rather than gently. Once the task is completed the bin is placed outside the therapy room, symbolically removing the anger from the room.

It is important to discuss with clients how they feel in terms of release of anger after this activity.

Writing for peace

You will need pens and paper for this exercise.

Discuss with your clients creatively expressing anger. Remind them that when expressing anger, it is not OK to hurt themselves or other people or to break property.

Explain to them about writing down their feelings, putting on paper their anger and frustration. Encourage them to write anger words or sentences about how they feel. Remind them that it may not be acceptable to say those words to a person they might be angry with.

Invite them to write in an angry way. Maybe they could use scribbly writing or press hard with the pen. Clients could use a thicker pen or a particular colour to help them express how they feel.

Give clients space and quietly observe them during this exercise. Keep your comments until aferwards.

When they have finished ask them about their thoughts and feelings during this exercise. Invite them to decide what they want to do with their writing. You could suggest that they might like to destroy it in some sort of way – ripping, tearing, shredding, cutting until it is like confetti and impossible to decipher, or going outside and burning it.

Celebrate together getting rid of all those angry feelings safely.

Recycling your anger

For this exercise you will need some clean recycling: plastic bottles, paper, cardboard boxes. (Avoid glass for safety reasons.)

Discuss with your clients the importance of safe release of anger.

Place the recycling on the floor and invite clients to decide how they would like to release their anger in a safe way using these items. Encourage them to be creative and to come up with ideas for themselves. These could include:

Plastic bottles – stamping, kicking, squeezing, squashing

Paper – squashing, squeezing, tearing, shredding

Cardboard boxes – smashing, punching, ripping, tearing

When clients have decided what to do with the recycling, invite them to experiment doing the exercise by making a noise with their mouth or doing it silently.

Afterwards talk about the benefits of releasing anger safely using recycling materials. Ask them which approach was most helpful to them: being quiet or vocalising their feelings.

This is a low-cost environmentally-friendly way of expressing anger. Every household produces recycling. Clients can be encouraged to do this on their own at home as well as in therapy sessions.

Painting away the stress

For this exercise you will need:

Large covering for floor or table
Paper of various colours and textures
Washable poster paints
Brushes
Kitchen roll
Washing facilities – a bowl with soap, water and a towel if you have no sink

Discuss with your clients about releasing stress and anger. Then talk together about how painting is a good way to express emotions, putting them on paper and getting them out of their system. Remind your clients that they do not have to be artistic or be able to draw to create a painting for anger release.

Invite clients to select the type of paper, colours and thickness of brushes. Would they like instead to use their finger or hands? Assure clients that they can wash before they leave the room in order to remove the evidence.

Give clients time to think exactly what the anger is and how they would like to express it. Don't rush in. This is the clients' time. Allow them time to reflect.

Facilitate clients while they are painting. Don't interrupt. Only speak if they speak to you. Observe their facial expressions while they are working. These might reveal what is going on underneath the surface.

When the painting is completed, talk together about how it felt and what they were thinking while they were doing the exercise. Ask them how they feel now and what emotional changes they will take with them. Consider photographing the painting for your client notes.

Finally, ask clients what they want to do with the painting.

Wake and shake

This is an exercise to encourage clients to be aware of anger they may be holding in their bodies. Through shaking hands and feet, arms and legs, clients are helped to become aware of tension in their body related to anger.

Invite clients to stand up and gently move their feet, shaking them gently to remove the tension. Next, clients lift their legs one at a time and shake them. Now they shake hands, wrists and arms.

Then ask them to move shoulders, rolling them forwards, then backwards, then up and down. Invite them to shrug their shoulders, deliberately letting go of the anger, with a deep breath.

The next stage is gently to roll the head from side to middle, then from the middle to the other side and back to the middle. (This is an important safety feature for head exercises.) They then put their chin down on their chest, turn one way and back to the middle, then the other way and back to the middle.

Clients then sit down and relax. Talk with them about relaxing muscles and joints and letting tension go. Encourage clients to take responsibility for themselves, to be aware of tensions and anger held in their body and to release them before they become a headache or an illness.

Breathe your troubles out

Discuss with your clients how holding in anger can cause tension in the body and even physical illness. Talk about the benefits of releasing anger gradually and safely.

Invite them to sit comfortably, relax and close their eyes if they want to. Here is a form of words you can use:

I would like you to breathe deeply and slowly. (PAUSE) Be aware of what is happening in your body. (PAUSE) Feel your chest rising and the air coming out of your nose. Feel your body relaxing. (PAUSE)

Be aware of your muscles. (PAUSE) Your heartbeat. (PAUSE) The blood coursing through your body taking oxygen and nutrients to your vital organs. (PAUSE)

As you breathe, let those angry thoughts and feelings be released. (PAUSE)

Now with a big sigh I invite you to come back to the here and now.

Encourage clients to take time at home to relax regularly and breathe their troubles out.

My peaceful place

This activity involves clients in first expressing anger using clay or playdough, then leaving the anger behind as they find a peaceful place.

Invite clients to use the clay in a way that helps them to express their anger. Some people might model the shape of a person or thing they are angry about, then destroy it. Other clients may simply bang the clay hard until their anger subsides.

The next stage involves a visualisation to help clients find a way of dissipating their anger and being at peace.

Here is a form of words to use:

Relax, get into a comfortable position and close your eyes if you want to. We are going on a journey.

How do you feel? (PAUSE) Are you excited or scared? (PAUSE) We are boarding a ship. (PAUSE) Are there a lot of people? Or are you all alone? (PAUSE)

The ship sets out to sea. (PAUSE) Soon all the noise from the harbour is left behind. All you can hear is the wind and the waves lapping against the side of the vessel. (PAUSE)

Occasionally a gull flies past. (PAUSE) The sun is shining and the sea is blue. (PAUSE)

As you sail further from the land you feel your anger and trouble being left behind. Slipping away. (PAUSE) How does this feel? (PAUSE) What is it like to be relaxed and free of your anger? (PAUSE) Stay and enjoy the feeling of freedom. (PAUSE)

Breathe deeply. Enjoy the smell of the sea. (PAUSE) Enjoy the peace of this place. (PAUSE) You can come back any time you want. (PAUSE) This peaceful scene is always waiting in your imagination. (PAUSE)

When you are ready, come back to the here and now. Open your eyes and look around the room. Now say what that experience of releasing anger and breathing in peace was like for you.

After the visualisation discuss with clients what the experience was like for them. Invite them to use this idea at home. For example, making bread at home will be welcomed by others and kneeding it is an acceptable activity for anger expression. The best bread is well-kneeded and could be a much-needed release of anger for the baker. Then the person can sit quietly and go back to that place of peace.

Punch away your troubles

Probably one of the most effective ways to express anger creatively is to use fists on an object that doesn't matter or doesn't hurt the person doing the punching. In our therapy room we usually have a punchbag and a pile of cushions that can be used for the purpose.

If you plan to work with clients in this way, it is important that they first warm up their muscles with simple stretching exercises. If this is not done they could end up by hurting themselves.

Punchbags come in various shapes and sizes. Many of them need to be used with boxing gloves and supported from strong beams. Much more practical for a therapy room is an inflatable punchbag, which can be used with bare fists. We buy ours from companies with sports departments.

Inflatable punchbags are filled with water in the base, which takes at least two people. The bulk of the punchbag is inflated with air and kept topped up until it is reasonably firm.

A pile of pillows can also be used for creative anger expression. Make sure there are enough cushions so that your clients don't injure their hands on the floor or table underneath. An alternative is to place a thick piece of heavy-duty foam (the kind used for settee seat cushions) under the softer cushions. At home they can punch pillows or cushions on a bed or settee.

It is important that clients remove jewellery and watches or else the punchbag could be punctured. It is also useful to assure clients (perhaps with a demonstration) that the punchbag doesn't hurt if it hits the person. If you are leading with a group, they can work in pairs, one each side of the punchbag (being careful that they don't 'accidentally' miss the punchbag and hit each other!).

Invite clients to close their eyes (if they want to) and focus on something that they are angry about or perhaps a person they have anger towards. Then they begin the punching (which could lead to kicking without shoes or headbutting).

As they express their anger, watch carefully to ensure that they aren't hurting themselves or holding their breath for too long. If they start smiling or becoming slack in their activity, encourage them to focus again on the source of their anger.

Afterwards talk with clients about what the experience of punching away their troubles was like for them.

Anger around the house

For this exercise you will need a broom and possibly a dustpan and brush.

Talk to clients about the benefits of vigorous exercise and being out of breath. Discuss how this can help to release anger safely and enable clients to feel better.

Using the broom, demonstrate 'soft' sweeping and discuss how this does little or nothing to release anger. Suggest vigorous sweeping with short, brisk strokes of the broom. Invite clients to have a turn.

Ask them how they experienced the activity.

Then discuss things they can do at home to release their anger in creative ways:

Energetic vacuuming – angrily removing all the dust from the floors.

Bathroom cleaning – stretching and bending, rubbing vigorously to eliminate all the germs.

Window and mirror cleaning – polishing the angry feelings away with enthusiastic arm movements.

Sorting cupboards – determinedly and angrily removing unwanted objects, tidying and bagging items for the charity shop or the recycling bins.

At the end of this clients will have the satisfaction of a clean house and they will feel better from the release of pent-up anger.

Bursting balloons

For this exercise you will need a packet of balloons. Talk with clients about safe anger expression.

Invite them to select balloons based on their colour and size. Some clients might identify a colour with anger while others might think a colour is too beautiful to associate with anger.

Decide how many balloons you will need, then together blow up the balloons ready for bursting. Discuss how clients would like to burst the balloons. Consider different ways:

Gently squeezing
Sitting on them
Jumping on them
Bursting them with a pin or scissors
Biting them
Blowing them up until they burst

Get clients to be creative and see how many ways of bursting balloons they can find.

Once some of the balloons have been burst, ask clients how it felt to do this. Encourage them to burst several balloons very quickly so that they are out of breath.

Spend time afterwards talking about the experience.

Touch and block

Anger expression doesn't always have to be a solitary task. You as the therapist can join with your clients in plenty of creative ways of expressing anger. If you are working with a group, the group members can work in pairs to express anger in what can prove to be effective and enjoyable ways.

The following activities involve working in pairs and require an element of physical contact. Many therapists struggle with the idea of touching their clients in any way. If you can overcome these barriers and use touch ethically and professionally, it can help clients who struggle alone with anger.

First, there is **attack and avoid,** an activity developed from judo. Each partner puts a hand on the other's shoulder and holds their elbow with the other hand. Then both use one foot to try to touch the other's foot. The act of 'attacking' and 'avoiding' makes for good fun and involves plenty of creative energy. Once both partners have mastered this activity, consider increasing the speed.

Shoulder pushing is another useful activity with the added element of competition. Partners stand side by side and make contact shoulder to shoulder. If one is taller than the other, the taller one bends down so that both are the same height. The idea is that partners push against each other as hard as they can.

Foot fight involves sitting on the floor, partners putting the bottoms of their shoes together and pushing as hard as they can. It is best to wear good, solid shoes for this.

With f**ace-to-face shoulder pushing** the partners put their hands on each other's shoulders, bend so they are both the same height, then push hard.

Finally, there is **touch and block.** Partners face each other and attempt to touch the other person's shoulders. At the same time they block the other person's hand with the blade (inside forearm) of one or the other arm. Speeding up the activity makes for plenty of creative anger expression.

After each of these activities in pairs discuss with clients how they feel in terms of letting go of their anger.

Sources and references

Berne, Eric (1975). *What Do You Say After You Say Hello?: The psychology of human destiny.* London: Corgi. (Original work published 1972.)

Bridle, Tina, & Sweet, Annie (2000). Anger: The oppressed emotion, in *ITA Conference Papers,* Canterbury: Institute of Transactional Analysis, pages 28-34.

Coleman, Vernon (1990). *Bodysense.* London: Sheldon Press.

Day, Roger (2004). *Being Mad, Being Glad.* Oxford: Raintree Publishers.

Day, Roger (2008). Creative play therapy with children and young people, in Tudor, Keith (2008). *The Adult is Parent to the Child: Transactional analysis with children and young people.* Lyme Regis: Russell House Publishing, pages 174-185.

Frazier, Tom (1995). Anger: Don't express it and don't repress it. *Transactional Analysis Journal, 25,* 2, pages 123-128

Jackson, Tim (2000). Can anger be positive? *Christian Counsellor, 5,* April-June 2000, pages 10-14.

McKay, Matthew, Rogers, Peter, & McKay, Judith (1989). *When Anger Hurts: Quieting the storm within.* Oakland, California: New Harbinger Publications.

Miller, Jonathan (2012). http://psychotherapysphere.com/anger-spotlight-shield-and-balloon

Nhât Hanh, Thich (2001). *Anger: Wisdom for cooling the flames.* New York: Riverhead books.

O'Connor, Joseph, & Seymour, John (1993). *Introducing Neuro-Linguistic Programming: Psychological skills for understanding and influencing people.* London: Aquarian Press. (Original work published 1990.)

Rude, Stephanie S, Chrisman, J G, Burton Denmark, A, Maestas, K L (2012). Expression of direct anger and hostility predict depression symptoms in formerly depressed women. *Canadian Journal of Behavioural Science/Revue canadienne des sciences du comportement.* Advance online publication. doi: 10.1037/a0027496

Sharratt, Zoe (2009). The messy stage in the therapeutic process. *Play for Life,* Summer 2009, pages 10-15.

Smith, Robert (2000). Personal communication. Rugby, Warwickshire.

Sound Feelings (2004). www.soundfeelings.com/feelanger.htm, 19/5/2012

Sunderland, Margot, & Engleheart, Philip (1993). *Draw on Your Emotions: Creative ways to explore, express and understand important feelings.* Bicester: Winslow Press.

Temple, Susannah (1993). Anger fuels effectiveness. *ITA News,* Summer 1993, pages 7-8.

Whitehouse, Èliane, & Pudney, Warwick (1996). *A Volcano in My Tummy: Helping children to handle anger.* Gabriola Island, British Columbia: New Society Publishers.

Widdowson, Mark (2008). Working with adolescents, in Tudor, Keith (2008). *The Adult is Parent to the Child: Transactional analysis with children and young people.* Lyme Regis: Russell House Publishing, pages 132-150.

Wilde, Jerry (1996). Treating Anger, Anxiety and Depression in Children and Adolescents. Washington, DC: Accelerated Development.

Printed in Great Britain
by Amazon